The Kardashians
A KRAZY LIFE
POSY EDWARDS

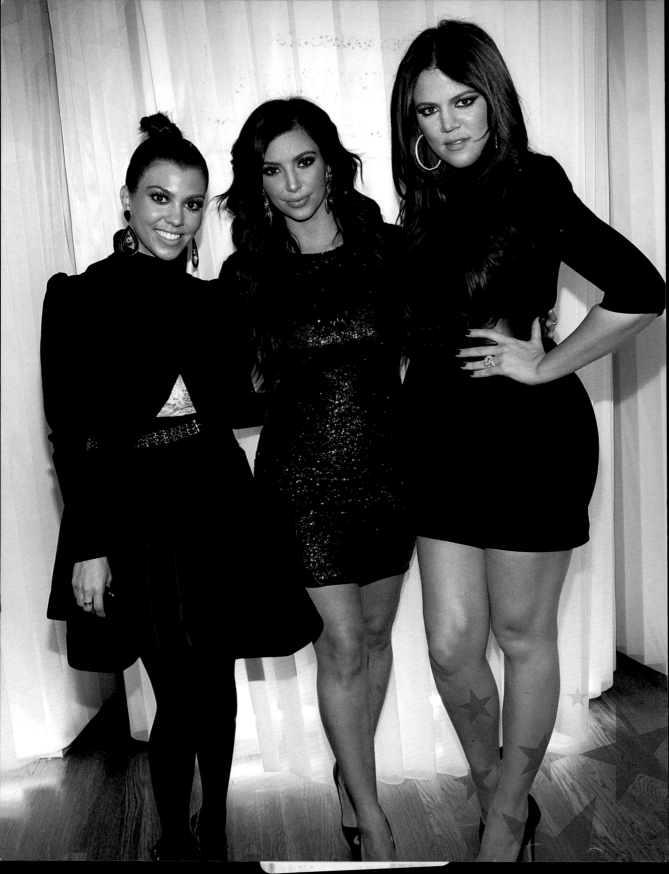

Introducing The Kardashians!

Unless you've been hiding under a rock for the past two years, you'll have heard the Kardashian name somewhere. The family's most famous export, Kim Kardashian, has been popping up in commercials and TV shows in the mid 2000s and since then the whole family has been catapulted to fame.

The gorgeous Kardashian sisters – Kim, older sis Kourtney and baby sis, Khloé – are now stars of their own reality TV show. Oh, and they also run a designer clothing empire called D-A-S-H, design clothes and jewellery collections, release their own perfume and date American pro footballers!

Those Dash dolls are super hot – but just how much do you know about their huge family? Read on to find out all the family's secrets – the cat-fights, break-ups and make-ups, as well as fashion, style and love advice from the most popular girls on the scene right now!

Meet The Kardashians!

Everyone recognises Kim – she was one of the most photographed faces on the planet in 2010! But how much do you really know about the person behind the beautiful face?

Kim's parents Robert and Kris were married in 1978, and had four children: Kourtney, Kim, Khloé and Robert Jr. The couple divorced in 1990, and Kris then married Bruce Jenner, an Olympic athlete. Bruce already had four kids from two previous marriages – Burt and Casey from his first marriage, and Brody and Brandon from his second marriage. Adding to this huge pool of children, Bruce and Kris then had two daughters – Kendall and Kylie. That's a whole lot of Christmas presents to remember!

Phew! Are you keeping up? Take a rest and check out the stats on the Kardashian kids – Kim, Kourtney, Khloé, and their little bro Rob!

Kim, Kourtney, Khloé and Rob are fourth generation Armenians, born and raised in Los Angeles. Their great-grandparents from their dad's side came to LA from Armenia. Their great-grandfather was Armenian and their great grandmother was Turkish-Armenian. Although mom Kris is half-Scottish and half-Dutch, the Kardashian kids grew up with a huge Armenian influence, always hearing stories of Armenia, eating Armenian food and celebrating Armenian holidays!

'My father would be so proud that we talk about our Armenian heritage!' says Kim. 'My dad used to always tell us to never remove the 'ian' from our last name like some Armenians that came to the US. He was so proud to be Armenian and his biggest regret was not sending us to Armenian school! I am so proud to be Armenian and so happy that I can identify with my Armenian fans!'

VITAL STATS

Kim Kardashian

Name: Kimberly Noel Kardashian

Birthday: 21 October 1980

Birthplace: Los Angeles, California

Starsign: libra

Height: 5 feet 3 inches

Hair colour: black

Eye colour: dark brown

Style icons: her mom, Gwen Stefani, Jennifer Lopez, Rihanna

Girl crushes: Megan Fox, Victoria Beckham

Favourite music: R & B, pop, hip hop, classic rock

Favourite colours: red and white

Favourite movies: *Clueless, The Notebook, The Rock, Beaches*

Favourite Christmas movies: *The Santa Clause, The Christmas Story, How the Grinch Stole Christmas, The Holiday, Home Alone*

Favourite TV shows: *Court TV, Forensic Files, Oprah, Extreme Makeover: Home Edition, Sex and the City, Dancing with the Stars*

Favourite foods: seafood, salads, sushi (but only certain types!)

Favourite sweets: deep-fried Oreos, ice cream and cookies, granola, sliced fruit

Favourite drink: she rarely drinks alcohol, but when she does she enjoys sipping on a White Russian

Favourite Armenian dish: Lamajune with string cheese

Favourite vacation destinations: if Kim is madly in love, Bora Bora. If it's just her and her girls, then anywhere. She loves Hawaii and St. Tropez

Three things she would take to a desert island: her BlackBerry, her computer and photos

Pet peeve: people who lie

Kim food fact: Famous Cupcakes in Los Angeles created a vanilla cupcake mix for Kim called Va-Va-Va-Nilla

Freaky Kim fact: she sleeps with her eyes slightly open

Crazy cash Kim fact: Kim was the highest earning reality TV star in 2010, earning over six million dollars! At least she can afford all those shopping trips…

'Kim is a princess. When we were little I was the older sister and the boss. I used to boss Kim around, but she would remain a princess. Kim is also very sweet. You don't necessarily always see this side of Kim on the show. They don't always show all the good stuff. They show Kim as the diva, and that's just one side to her. For the most part, Kim is very sweet and generous. Kim has a princess mindset. She wants a prince charming, that's what she believes in. Kim also gets whatever she wants.'

— Kourtney

'Kourtney is the most loyal and responsible person I know.' — Kim

10

VITAL STATS

Kourtney Kardashian

Name: Kourtney Mary Kardashian

Birthday: 18 April 1979

Birthplace: Los Angeles, California

Starsign: pisces

Height: 5 feet

Hair colour: black

Eye colour: dark brown

Schooling: she attended the University of Arizona and graduated with a degree in Theatre Arts and Spanish

Favourite cities: Monaco, Florence, Milan, Venice and Miami

Favourite foods: any junk food, Sour Cream & Onion Lays, Milk Duds, bagels with cream cheese

Favourite ways to pass time: Kourtney is a mall rat – she loves spending time in inexpensive fun stores. She always visits Forever 21, Zara, H&M and Sephora

Favourite magazines: *Elle Décor, Architectural Digest, Elle* and *Bazaar*

Favourite TV shows: *Lost, American Idol, Keeping Up With The Kardashians!*

Favourite thing: when her son Mason smiles at her

Time she was starstruck: when she met Michael Jackson

Travelling: Kourtney's least favourite thing about travelling is packing – it takes her hours!

Strange fact: Kourtney can sleep anywhere, in airports, on planes, in cars – anywhere!

VITAL STATS

Khloé Kardashian

Name: Khloé Alexandra Kardashian

Birthday: 27 June 1984

Birthplace: Calabasas, California

Starsign: cancer

Height: 5 feet 10 inches

Hair colour: dark brown

Eye colour: green/hazel

Beauty icons: Cindy Crawford, Rihanna

Favourite feature: her eyes and eyelashes

Favourite movies: *Drop Dead Fred*, *Little Shop of Horrors*

Favourite magazines: *Life & Style*, *Vogue*, and *Hip-Hop Weekly*

Favourite TV shows: *The Real Housewives* of any city, *Keeping Up With The Kardashians*, and *Divine Design*

Favourite music: she loves all types of music; Carrie Underwood, Lil Wayne, Young Jeezy, Keri Hilson, Drake, Rihanna, Taylor Swift, Miley Cyrus, The Pussycat Dolls, Pink … the list goes on!

Style icons: Mary Kate and Ashley Olsen, Jackie O, Audrey Hepburn, Victoria Beckham and Rihanna

Being starstruck: when she met Rihanna for the first time

Crazy hair fact: when she was a child, Khloé's hair was blonde and curly!

'Khloé definitely has the biggest heart and she's super understanding.' — Kim

'I would say Khloé is definitely hilarious and funny. One thing people don't know about Khloé is that she is super sensitive . . . and would do anything for any of us. If anyone would say something bad about me she would be extremely protective.' — Kourtney

VITAL STATS

Rob Kardashian

The Kardashians have four family dogs: Dolce (boy Chihuahua), Gabanna (girl Labrador), Bella (girl Maltese) and Butter (girl Boxer). Kim shares Butter with her sister Khloé. 'We've always had dogs!' says Kim. 'My dad always loved pure breeds and wanted the best so he always had Dobermans when we were growing up. I think dogs are great to be around and such a valuable part of the family.'

Name: Robert Arthur Kardashian Jr

Birthday: 17 March 1987

Birthplace: Los Angeles, California

Starsign: pisces

Height: 5 feet 11 inches

Hair colour: black

Eye colour: dark brown

Schooling: Rob attended the University of Southern California and graduated with nearly the highest marks in his class

Relationships: dated Cheetah Girl Adrienne Bailon between 2008 and 2009 but currently single

Dash half-sisters Kylie and Kendall are keeping up the Dash doll tradition of being totally gorgeous – both sisters have started modelling and are wowing the public!

Kris and Bruce Jenner

Mom Kris acts as manager for her hugely talented Kardashian daughters, while stepdad Bruce is a regular feature on *Keeping Up With The Kardashians* as the confused father surrounded by a house of crazy women!

Growing up as a Kardashian

School's Out!

Kim, Kourtney and Khloé all attended Marymount High School, an exclusive girls-only Catholic school on Sunset Boulevard in LA, the same school that their mom Kris went to. High school was fun, though the girls suffered the same trials and tribulations that all girls go through at school. Khloé was teased for her weight, and Kim was the first girl in her class who started to develop physically.

Kim was also teased for her off-the-wall fashion choices. 'In school, there were many things that happened where my confidence was taken away by girls being mean,' she says. 'Everyone gets teased at

KIM FACT:

Kim would freak out if she had to eat her lunch alone in high school! 'If my friends were in different classes or I couldn't find them at lunch time — I would shake,' she says.

school at some point or another, including me. The important thing is to be proud of your style – no matter what!'

But really, Kim never suffered at the hands of bullies – she always got along with everyone. 'I was always cool with all the different cliques and made sure just to be nice to everyone,' she says.

All three sisters were at Marymount at the same time, but there was a strong sense of sibling rivalry between Kourtney and Kim, who were only 18 months apart in age. Back then, the sisters were super competitive. 'As kids we'd fight over clothes, and friends – everything!' says Kourtney.

One thing the girls did share in common was a love of fashion and style. 'My mom definitely taught us at a young age to care about our appearances. She taught me how to shave my legs!' says Kourtney. Mom Kris had a collection of special YSL compacts, and the girls used to love going through mom's drawers and checking out all her makeup.

How To Handle High School

'I am a very positive person and I think you should treat others how you would want to be treated. And just be a nice person. And if that's how you are, I think it would be easier to handle high school life.' — Khloé

Sisterly love

Even though they may have fought each other, the sisters were always close. When it came time for Kourtney and Kim to leave high school, baby sis Khloé was suddenly faced with the prospect of having to finish school while her sisters weren't there.

'I felt like I didn't have any friends. There was no reason for me to stay,' says Khloé. So she forged some paperwork, located a homeschool, went there and enrolled herself. She managed to convince her parents that she belonged there, and brainy Baby K managed to finish three years of high school in one year – and graduated when she was 17, with honours! 'So in your face,' she says!

Forging paperwork wasn't the only trouble Khloé got up to as a youngster. 'I was a major trouble maker,' she says. She even stole her mom's car once and accidentally set it on fire! Even though she's still a firecracker these days, Khloé has learned to channel her destructive energies into her work.

BEING RESPONSIBLE

'When I was about 15 my dad would take me driving with him every weekend to make sure I was prepared to get behind the wheel. He made me make a promise to him that, no matter what, I had to go out with my sister Kourtney and her friends, because he knew they were a little older than me and they may be drinking. I promised him I would always drive them home, and no matter what time it was, I had to call him to let him know we made it to our friends' houses safe and sound if we slept out. I always wanted to make him proud!' — Kim

Growing up – the Kardashian way

Mom Kris and dad Rob (and later stepdad Bruce) were very positive influences on their children. Even though the kids were raised in a wealthy family and around a world of celebrity, mom Kris was adamant that the children all had to find their own way in life and not sponge off their parents.

'My father taught us really well, and I think really instilled a good work ethic in us,' says Kim. 'We didn't have the credit cards. We didn't have the cell phones. We didn't have that, like all of our friends did, growing up.'

When all the Kardashian kids turned 18, they didn't get any handouts from mom, and had to seek out work. So even though Kim received a car for her sweet 16th birthday, when she reached 18 – she was cut off!

Throughout high school Kim had worked for her dad's music marketing firm, Movie Tunes, and it was through that and their other celebrity connections she ended up befriending other socialites like Paris and Nicky Hilton and Nicole Richie.

'I lead a very positive life,' says Kim. 'My parents brought us up to focus on the positive and so I try not to let any negativity in. I keep positive people around me, have an amazing family and group of friends.'

TOP TIP FOR GETTING THROUGH HIGH SCHOOL

'Confidence. If I had the confidence I had now when I was in high school, I swear I'd own the school. I just think having confidence and being secure in yourself is the main thing.'
— Kourtney

Life after school

After high school, bright spark Kourtney decided she wanted to go to college to get her degree. She enrolled in the University of Arizona and moved there to study Theatre Arts and Spanish. After her course was finished, she and mom Kris embarked on their first business venture together, and opened a children's fashion store called Smooch in California.

The call of love

Still at home, middle sister Kim wondered what was the right path for her. But it was love that decided her fate. She met and fell in love with music producer Damon Thomas, and even though she was only 20 years old the couple decided to get married. But there were rocky times ahead – in 2003 Kim's dad Robert Kardashian Senior died from cancer, and then in 2004 Kim and Damon split up, and went through what must have been a difficult time.

Luckily for Kim, she had her finely-honed style skills to pull her through. Her friend, R&B singer Brandy, had appeared on a Worst Dressed list, and was devastated. So she hired Kim as a stylist to help her get her wardrobe in order.

Kim answered her life's calling as a wardrobe stylist, working on music videos, TV shows and fashion photo shoots. Her strong sense of style, ambition and drive led to a job as personal shopper and stylist for celebrity clients like Paris and Nicky Hilton, Nicole Richie and Lindsay Lohan. Sweet work if you can get it!

Employing Kim's entrepreneurial business skills, she started on her own as a fashion stylist and became a sought after wardrobe stylist for infomercials, television shows, music videos and photo shoots. But it was her super sense of organisation, arrangement and construction of high fashion closets that led her into a unique line of work – overhauling and designing closets for celebrities. Wow!

D-A-S-H

The three sisters knew they had the strength and determination to succeed at whatever they wanted to do. Kourtney had finished university and Khloé had finished school. With their combined energy and fashion and style sense, it seemed like the most sensible thing to do was to open a clothes store. Their grandma MJ had owned a children's clothes store for 30 years – that was the inspiration behind opening Smooch – but the girls wanted to do their own thing: fashionable clothes for grown ups!

After hours and hours of plotting and planning their dream store space, the original D-A-S-H store opened in 2006 in their hometown of Casabalas in California. The theme for the store was eclectic, glamorous and flirty fashions, and attracted famous customers like Paris Hilton and Nicole Richie. The store even featured its own lines of jeans and Armenian-style inspired jewellery designed by the talented sisters.

The California store was so popular that the Dash dolls opened another two stores, one in Miami, and another in New York! You might think that all the success would have gone to their heads with the three stores, but actually they are really involved in running the businesses.

They even got their hands dirty when it came to putting the D-A-S-H stores together. Stepdad Bruce and Kourtney would get up at 6am everyday to go to pick up supplies, then head to D-A-S-H and put up the mouldings and build the dressing rooms. A multi-talented family indeed!

After TV executives realised that the Kardashian-Jenner tribe was already a real life soap opera, they offered the family a reality TV show, with Kim at its centre. The show was called *Keeping Up With The Kardashians*, and followed the adventures of the Dash sisters and Rob Junior, as well as mom and stepdad Kris and Bruce and all the half and step brothers and sisters of the family. There was a lot to take in!

At first the TV execs were nervous – they didn't know whether the show would be a hit or not. But they didn't need to worry. *Keeping Up With The Kardashians* became one of the most popular reality shows on TV, with millions of viewers, and it catapulted the family into megastardom!

THE FIRST PAPARAZZI SCARE

'I was lying out on the beach in Miami on New Year's Eve, and, like, 50 paparazzi started gathering. I was like, "Who's here . . . JLo?" But they started hounding me! I wasn't used to that at all — I had to go back into my hotel.'
— Kourtney

23

Love and Romance

The Kardashian sisters have had their ups and downs in terms of romance – they know about the joys of being in love, but they know about heartbreak too!

Kim

Despite being wrongly romantically linked with almost every hot, young single male on the planet Kim is actually a very loyal girlfriend who prefers long-term relationships to anything casual.

After meeting and falling in love with record producer Damon Thomas, Kim decided to get married when she was just 20 years old! But the marriage was difficult and the couple went through a messy divorce four years later. Kim enjoyed being single after meeting New Orleans Saints running back Reggie Bush but didn't want to play the field anymore. The couple had a fairytale romance, with flowers, extravagant gifts, spontaneous holiday breaks, and the whole thing documented on *Keeping Up With The Kardashians*!

Unfortunately, the strain of Kim's professional life was too much for the couple. They briefly split in 2009, but got back together after sister Khloé's wedding. 'It takes a lot to be in a long distance relationship especially when the both of us have so much going on,' Kim said. And even though they tried spending more time together, it wasn't to be, and they ended their relationship for good in early 2010.

'I want to try to be single,' says Kim. 'I've never just dated and done whatever I wanted. I have a hundred different jobs — when do I have time to really focus on someone? I've made a promise to myself and I'm really trying hard to stick to it, but I'm such a hopeless romantic that it's hard. I don't think that's going to last, because that's just how I am. But the fact that I'm trying is a big step for me!'

Kim's relationship tip

'My biggest relationship tip is to trust your heart, learn to compromise and always be honest. A lot of the time you can lose sight of things when you start letting other people into your relationship. Everyone wants to be involved, or give their two cents on the situation, but only you really know the ins and outs of the relationship.' — Kim

There were plenty of rumours of the couple getting back together – but Kim was adamant she was going to forget boys and concentrate on work.

Perhaps the most controversial love rumour that's circulated about Kim since the split from Reggie is that her and JUSTIN BIEBER are an item! The pair did a photoshoot together for ELLE and became BBM buddies – which inspired death threats for Kim from some of Justin's hardcore fans! Luckily for the Biebettes, Kim and Justin are just good friends. Phew!

The rumour mill ground to a halt in summer 2011, when Kim announced that she would be marrying Kris Humphries, a basketball star. The couple had been dating for just six months, but both Kris and Kim were certain: the love-struck groom tweeted 'This is it!'. Eva Longoria, Lindsay Lohan, Mel B and Avril Lavigne were among the 440 guests at the dream wedding in California, where Kim wore a fabulous bespoke dress by Vera Wang. The wife-to-be made a touching tribute to her late dad before going on to say 'I do' to the other most important man in her life.

Kourtney

One of the main ongoing stories in *Keeping Up With The Kardashians* has been the constant on/off relationship between Kourtney and her partner Scott Disick.

Scott grew up in Long Island and went to The Ross School, an exclusive private school. He often rubbed shoulders with high-flying socialites, so he was right at home with Kourtney as soon as they met!

But Kourtney wasn't happy with Scott's party-hard lifestyle. She went through several moments of clarity – even breaking up with him before she moved to Miami with Khloé to open another D-A-S-H store. But she and Scott met up soon after that, and Kourtney fell pregnant!

Since getting pregnant, Kourtney made much more of an effort to include Scott in her life, as did the rest of her family. But a few members – especially Kris and little sis Khloé – were outspoken in putting Scott down, believing he wasn't good enough for Kourtney.

The birth of their son, Mason Dash Disick, seemed to have inspired a change for the better in Scott's life. But still Scott couldn't seem to keep it together, and on an episode of *Keeping Up With The Kardashians* he was seen smashing a mirror and slamming a bathroom door. Kourtney even left Scott for a few weeks after a fight in where he smashed bottles, punched walls and ended up in the hospital's emergency room.

This led the whole Kardashian family to serious worry about Kourtney and baby Mason.

But away from the cameras, Scott started rehabilitation for his drinking, surprising everyone, including mom Kris. 'I think Scott has definitely done a 180,' she says. 'He's matured over the last year in the way he's treated Kourtney and he's the best dad.'

As for whether Kourtney and Scott will last the distance, no-one knows. But Kourtney now says that she has the one love of her life to focus on – and that is baby Mason! All the other boys come in a close second to her son.

Kourtney's First Kiss

'My best friend and I went to sleep-away camp every summer. We'd share stories of making out with boys, but we never did, so we made it all up. My real first kiss was at a friend's house when I was in junior high. He was such a good kisser, and we're still close friends!' — Kourtney

Khloé

Khloé was never that bothered about relationships when she was younger. She even hosted an anti-Valentine Day party one year! So it was a huge surprise when – after dating Lamar Odom for just a month – the couple decided to get married!

Mom Kris was completely shocked. 'Khloé never brought a boy home to say hello, and in five minutes she was engaged and I had nine days to plan a wedding,' she says!

Although some people said the quickie wedding was planned because of the show and to create some drama for the cameras, Khloé dismissed that, enjoying the whirlwind of the romance.

Khloé and Lamar were married in front of family and friends, against a backdrop of arches of white roses. Khloé was dressed in a gorgeous white Vera Wang wedding dress, and she walked down the aisle with stepdad Bruce and her sisters Kim and a very pregnant Kourtney beside her!

The wedding was held at the home of a family friend. Over 250 guests turned up – and all of them were banned from using BlackBerrys at the ceremony! The bridesmaids were Kim and Kourtney, half-sisters Kendall and Kylie Jenner, actresses (and twin sisters) Khadijah and Malika Haqq and actress Lauren London, who were all dressed in gorgeous lavender gowns and were carrying bouquets of white roses.

Khloé's whirlwind romance and marriage was a complete change for Baby K, who had previously always been single while Kim and Kourtney were in relationships.

Khloé's love tip - How to get your crush to notice you

'I also think if you try too hard for your crush to notice you, you look like a fool. I think just be who you are and if he doesn't notice you then he's not the one for you and there's a reason for that. Sometimes, people have a crush because everyone hypes this person up and then when you hang out with them you're like, "Ooh, you're so lame." You're not even a nice person. And if you're yourself and he doesn't like you, then move on and find a new crush cause honey, there are millions of new crushes. Don't change for anybody.' — Khloé

Katwalk Kardashians

If there's one thing the Kardashian sisters are known for, it's their impeccable sense of style, fabulous dress sense and their picture perfect make-up and hair. It helps, of course, that mom Kris is drop-dead gorgeous, and that dad Rob Kardashian Senior gave their girls his smouldering dark Armenian looks. But there are plenty of fashion tips and secrets that the girls have learned along the way – and want to share with you!

Natural Beauty

Although the Kardashian sisters were definitely born with good genes, they all understand the importance of working out and looking after yourself. Living with an Olympic champion (stepdad Bruce) will do that to you!

Body Confidence

Kim may love her gorgeous curvy figure now – but back when she was younger, her shape made her cry! 'I was the first girl in my class to wear a bra. I remember crying in the bathtub. All my friends were super-skinny,' she says. But having some heart-to-hearts with mom Kris soon meant that Kim saw sense. Mom Kris told her that she had curves and that would never change, so she better start embracing them. And embrace them she did!

Kim showed how serious she was about exercise when she released an video designed for toning up and staying in shape for curvy girls! 'For young girls to see exercise videos that have only skinny girls… well, that's something they can't attain,' Kim says. 'I want this to be something that can be realistic for most girls.'

Work Out!

Although all three sisters work out, it's oldest sister Kourtney who does the least exercise. Kourtney had always been tiny throughout her whole life – in fact, when she was in kindergarten she had to get special school uniforms made because she was still wearing in baby sizes! 'But she knows working out isn't just to lose weight, it's to maintain a healthy lifestyle,' says Kim.

All three Kardashian sisters work out to achieve their gorgeous hourglass figures, and they love it – they don't see it as a chore at all, and they're realistic about embracing their curves rather than starving themselves to be super skinny. 'I have cellulite, just like almost every other woman on the planet,' says Kim.

Although Kim and Kourtney are fairly similar in shape and size, younger sister Khloé was definitely blessed in the height department – at 5 feet 10 inches, she towers above older sis Kourtney! But she's not shy about her height – far from it.

Kim's Top Ten Songs for working out!

Check out this awesome mixtape – exactly what Kim listens to for getting her pumped at the gym!

'Love Sex Magic' by Ciara
'Your Love is My Drug' by Ke$ha
'Since U Been Gone' by Kelly Clarkson
'Crazy in Love' by Beyonce
'California Gurls' by Katy Perry
'Bulletproof' by La Roux
'Telephone' by Lady Gaga
'Baby' by Justin Bieber
'OMG' by Usher
'Here We Go Again' by Demi Lovato

Healthy Eating Helps

All three Dash sisters changed their diets from eating things like cheeseburger and cheese-smothered enchiladas to healthy salads and shakes. The one sister who finds this more difficult is Kourtney – the self-confessed junk food addict!

Make-up Like a Kardashian

As kids, the Kardashian sisters went to an all girls Catholic school where they had to wear uniforms, so the only way they could express themselves was by wearing cute shoes or with lipstick.

'I remember wearing lipstick in seventh grade!' says Kourtney. 'Our teacher would take our lipsticks away and throw them away every day. That's why we would buy cheap lipsticks. It was a burgundy colour lipstick. Not a cute colour. We also then began wearing eyeliner.'

Learn Like a Pro

At home, stylish mom Kris was collecting limited edition MAC compacts, and Kourtney and Kim used to love going through her make-up and putting it on secretly in the mirror. Later, when mom Kris and dad Rob got divorced, their dad's new fiancée was also into make-up and got make-up lessons for Kim and Kourtney as a surprise! The girls loved the lessons and learned a lot from them.

Kim says that one of the most important things about make-up is to allow your make-up style to change over the years. 'I used to love heavy make-up and smokier eyes, and wouldn't really try new looks. Now, I will try anything and love fresh, lighter looks,' she says.

Although they've been papped without make-up on, the girls rarely go out in public with naked faces. They are all about the glamour! As for their must-have make-up products, Kim's favourite is MAC lipstick, she wears it all day long. Kourtney can't be without hairspray, and Khloé hates shine, so she always has a compact with powder.

Kardashian beauty routines

Kim: 'If I'm having a casual day, I put on tinted moisturizer and some blush and I'm ready!'

Kourtney: 'At night-time before going out I take about an hour to get ready. In the mornings I take 30 minutes. I'm pretty low maintenance.'

Khloé: 'I wear less make-up in the daytime — I never wear foundation in the daytime unless I'm doing an appearance. Mascara is a must for me — I always do mascara, a little bit of blush and lips and fill in my eyebrows and I'm good to go.'

10 ⭐ Steps to Kardashian make-up beauty!

Step 1 – Keep your skin clean!

This is vital to reduce breakouts and keep your skin as healthy as it can be. Make sure you remove all make-up before bed and wash your face thoroughly. Remember to moisturise too!

Step 2 – Prime-tastic

Use a facial primer – foundation primers work well – to condition the skin before you apply make-up.

Step 3 – Foundation

To avoid any shine, use a matte foundation and blend it into your skin with a foundation brush.

Step 4 – Conceal those dark circles

Everyone has dark circles under their eyes sometimes. Use a brightening concealer product under the eyes to hide the evidence of any late nights!

Step 5 - Powder

Set your face with translucent powder, again to reduce any shine. Dust your brush with a little of the powder then gently apply across your whole face.

Step 6 - Eyebrows

Make sure they're tweezed and fill them in using an eyebrow pencil.

Step 7 - Eyes

You need to pick your eye shadow depending on your own skin colouring and also your style. You need a base colour that you apply all over the lid. Then on the outer corners of the eyes, along the crease and along the lower lash line you apply a darker smoky colour. Then on the inner rim of the eye and along the brow bone, you apply a lighter highlight colour. Line the bottom and top of the eyelid with black eyeliner, curl your lashes and apply generous sweeps of mascara.

Step 8 - Cheeks

Apply matte bronzers to the hollow of your cheeks to highlight your gorgeous cheekbones. Make sure you use matte bronzers, which will stop shine and any possible muddy effects.

Step 9 - Dazzle

Use a highlighting powder to apply to your cheekbone and the bridge of your nose.

Step 10 - Lips

Line your lips using a lip liner, then fill them in using a slightly lighter shade of lipstick. Finally add a slick of gloss to make your lips really pop, Kardashian style!

And voila! You are picture perfect. Now where's the red carpet?

Strut It Girls

The Dash girls make their bread and butter from knowing what's what on the catwalk, so it's no surprise their fashion sense is pretty well developed. Whatever the season, you'll always see these three gorgeous sisters rocking the current trends – or breaking new ones! The girls all owe a lot to their celebrity stylist Monica Rose, who's always on hand – whatever the weather – to make sure there's not a hair out of place.

'Fashion is about creativity and expressing yourself! Go for it people!' — Khloé

FACTFILE

Kim's favourites

Clothes: Dolce & Gabanna, Roberto Cavalli

Bags: Chanel, Balenciaga

Shoes: Christian Louboutin, Jimmy Choo

If Kim could only wear one designer for the rest of her life: 'American Apparel. Their designs are cute, edgy and stylish – but are still SO comfortable at the same time.'

When it comes to fashion, Kim is definitely all about looking good – she's rarely seen in leisurewear, even after a long flight! She loves wearing nude colours like beige. She's big on accessorising her outfits, going that extra mile to match shoes, cute clutches and jewellery. She loves vintage items, especially women's t-shirts that she has borrowed from her mom, and she mixes these vintage items with modern clothes to create a trendy updated vintage look.

Kourtney

So what about older sis, Kourtney? Well, her fashion style is all about looking chic but being comfortable. She is always looking for stylish flats that she can run around in, although she loves cute heels too. In fact, she spends the majority of her fashion budget just on shoes! She says that big sunglasses have saved her life, especially on days when she just doesn't have time for make-up. That's a great tip!

In the daytime, Kourtney wears jeans or shorts more than skirts or dresses as it's easier to get down on the floor and play with Mason that way. 'I'm all about throwing on some jean shorts and a white t shirt and not spending as much time getting ready... for now anyways,' she says!

And as for Kourtney's must have fashion item? 'The perfect white boyfriend button down shirt. Classic, amazing with jeans, pants, shorts, even over a bikini open with the sleeves rolled up!'

Khloé

Baby K has always had a bigger frame than her sisters, but she loves her shape and doesn't let it put her off wearing the latest styles.

As the more outspoken of the sisters, this is definitely reflected in her style. Her favourite trend is rock chick with lashings of glam. Khloé has gorgeous long legs, so she can often be seen rocking mini and micro dresses with towering heels. Her current favourite fashion trends are plaid headbands, feathers and fringe! 'Whether on my head, forehead or on my clothes, they are so cute. They bring a little hippie style out of you. Even if you're just wearing some jeans and a t-shirt, you can wear these things to add an adorable detail,' says Khloé.

Accessorise!

Like her sisters, Khloé is a sucker for good accessories – she frequently matches nail polish shades to her bag or bracelets, and loves wearing chic footwear. And when it comes to swimwear, Khloé doesn't hide under a cover up – she gets on her suit and flaunts her stuff! 'When you have a bigger butt, bottoms without ties on the side sometimes will cut into your skin. I have a booty, so I like ties because I can loosen them up a little,' she says. 'So if you have a little tummy, you can hide it.'

Khloé also likes to step out of her comfort zone occasionally and try items that she'd never normally wear. 'When I am at the store, I see the new things come in and sometimes there are some things that are so cute, yet I am not sure if it's very me. I know a lot of people feel that way. But why?' she asks. 'We should all definitely step out of the box sometimes and try new things. We don't know unless we try ladies! I, for one, happen to be very classic and try to mix in some fun things from time to time.'

If Khloé could wear just one designer for the rest of her life, it would be Alexander Wang.

Keeping Up With Those Kardashians!

The Kardashian-Jenner family started being followed around by cameras back in late 2007. And no-one, least of all the Dash sisters, had any idea how popular the TV series was going to be. Kim thought it would be cancelled after one season, and little sis Khloé wondered who on earth would want to watch the everyday life of her boring family!

Little did they know that the world was soon to become obsessed with the sisters, their celebrity friends, their fights, making-up, partying, boyfriends, and their day-to-day glitzy lifestyle!

Kardashians: Fact or Fiction?

Although some people think the show is scripted, according to central character Kim, what appears on camera is what happens in real life. 'Unfortunately our lives really are that insane!' she laughs. 'I think that's why people love the show so much. You can't fake the dynamic between us ... and people see how real we are, how much we all love each other and are there for each other.'

As for people who say the show is just a money-making scheme, the family disagree. 'We do the show 'cause we're happy and it's fun for us,' said Khloé Kardashian. Mum Kris jokes that they'll still be going at Season 52 – with youngest daughter Kylie's wedding!

'We're definitely not your average family, and there's always a little drama going on, but that's what makes life interesting!'
— Kim

'I love doing the show and I love filming it with my family. I think we're so lucky to be able to do it all together. There are definitely benefits and fun times, and we all get to experience so much.' — Kourtney

Quiet Time

But it's not all fun and games, being famous – sometimes it gets a little too much and the Kardashian sisters crave some peace and quiet. 'I love going to the mall and the grocery store in Calabasas, getting my nails done and no one cares or notices anything I'm doing,' says oldest sis Kourtney.

However much of a drag it is being massively famous and recognised everywhere, there are a lot of plus points to doing the show: the main part is that the family get to spend so much time together!

'Hanging out with your family at the show almost forces you to deal with issues that come up,' says Kourtney. 'Keeping Up With The Kardashians forces me to deal with my feelings. I don't know if I could do this if it wasn't with my family though. The show brings our family so much closer!'

Season 1

Season 1 was the introduction to the crazy life of the Kardashian-Jenners, and it smashed onto our screens with episodes that focused on the Kardashian sisters, but also featured manager-mom Kris, stepdad Bruce and half-sisters Kylie and Kendall. Bruce's other kids made appearances too, but really, it was Kim, Kourtney and Khloé who made the season so addictive. The cameras followed landmark occasions in Kim's life, as she prepared for her first big TV interview, almost fired her mom as her manager, and got into fights with her sisters. Mom Kris made big moves in this season, as she hired an unsuitable nanny, bought daughter Kendall a puppy, and taught Khloé and Kourtney to be compassionate when they found a homeless man living behind the D-A-S-H store in California.

Spin Offs

Keeping Up With The Kardashians spawned two spin-off series. The first was Kourtney and Khloé Take Miami, where the sisters left LA to open a new D-A-S-H store in Miami. The second spin-off was Kourtney and Kim Take New York, which followed the two sisters – plus baby Mason and on-off partner Scott – as they hit the Big Apple to open another branch of D-A-S-H! "So excited for some fall in the Big Apple," said Kourtney. 'No better place ... Are you ready, NYC?'

Season 2

The second season of the show focused more on the developing careers of Kim, Kourtney and Khloé. The girls also took self defence classes, went on an at-first unsuccessful family vacation, got into a lot (like, really, a lot!) of fights, and travelled to New Orleans to visit some parts of the city that were devastated by Hurricane Katrina. Younger brother Rob fell in love with ex-Cheetah Girl Adrienne Bailon and considered dropping out of college to pursue a modelling career, while mom/manager Kris tried to keep the family together, and made sure her girls were making shrewd business decisions!

Season 3

The drama continued into Season 3 of the show when – in early 2009 – Khloé got a prison sentence for driving while under the influence of alcohol, as she had difficulty coping with the anniversary of her father's death. It was a crazy time for Baby K, who also did a nude campaign for PETA, had a skin cancer test, and thought she might be adopted so got a DNA test! The family were worried about Kim's out-of-control shopping, and the middle Dash sister had to undergo eye surgery just before performing with the Pussycat Dolls. Kourtney went through continual problems with partner Scott, who was suspected of cheating on her – and the final episode revealed the heartbreak of both Kourtney and Khloé, dealing with ending relationships as Khloé was cheated on by boyfriend Rashad.

Season 4

Aired in late 2009, the fourth season of The Kardashians kicked off with surprise bonanza first episode The Wedding! Even though they had only been dating for a month, Khloé decided to get married to NBA star Lamar Odom. The family was against the hasty decision, but headstrong Baby K ignored them and got married anyway. After the wedding Kim realised she was missing ex Reggie Bush, and rekindled their relationship. In the season, Kim found a stray Chihuahua and was devastated when she had to give it up. She also had to heed a serious warning about her health after fainting, realising she had to stop taking on so much. Baby bro Rob tried to relight the flame for his ex Adrienne, but failed. Kourtney and Scott also had couple trouble, and tried to work through the issues of their relationship. Scott failed to take Kourtney's pregnancy seriously, and apologised, after realising he was in danger of losing Kourtney and his baby. Kourtney gave birth to a bouncing baby boy, who they called Mason Dash Disick.

Season 5

Shot in 2010, Season 5 followed Kim as she moved into her new house, which was christened with a food fight by her feisty family, much to her dismay! As a newly single woman, Kim got set up on a blind date, developed a crush on her new bodyguard, and partied with football star Miles Austin, making ex Reggie Bush hugely jealous, but she ended up breaking it off with Miles anyway. Kim also had a beauty shocker when a she suffered the horrible side effects of Botox and the skin around her eyes turned purple. Kim swore she would never get another injection again! The situation between Kourtney and Scott was just as heated as in the other seasons when Kourtney became obsessed with getting pregnant again, but Scott wasn't so keen and resisted. None of the Kardashian-Jenners turned up to Scott's birthday party in Las Vegas, so an angry Kourtney threatened to move away and started house hunting in New York. The girls discovered Kris smoking and helped her to stop. Feeling like she was out of shape, Kris hired a personal trainer but flirting between the two led to a huge row with Bruce. The Dash sisters toyed with the idea of expanding the D-A-S-H franchise by moving to New York.

Season 6

Season 6 airs in 2011 – and promises that the emotional rollercoaster of life with the Kardashian-Jenners will roll on – with some huge surprises in store!

'We have a really good time doing what we're doing. We love every project that we're into. We're just having a good time.' — Kim

VITAL STATISTICS

In terms of viewing figures, Season 4 was massive! The first episode of Season 4 - The Wedding – was the highest rated episode in the history of *The Kardashians*, with 3.2 million viewers! Then the second episode in Season 4 topped that – with an amazing 4.1 million viewers. Amazing!

The Future for the Kardashians

When you consider their awesome list of achievements, it's almost impossible to imagine what on earth could be next for the Kardashian sisters. Hopeless romantic Kim continues her search for Prince Charming – but is trying to focus on work. She was the highest paid reality TV star in the world in 2010, but considering the size of her shopping sprees, she needs to be!